THOUGHTFUL
REFLECTIONS

THOUGHTFUL REFLECTIONS

A Treasury Of Spiritually Inspired Poems

Worrel A. Edwards

authorHOUSE®

AuthorHouse™
1663 Liberty Drive
Bloomington, IN 47403
www.authorhouse.com
Phone: 1-800-839-8640

Scripture Quotations are taken from the King james Version (KJV) of the Bible-Public Domain

Published by AuthorHouse   01/08/2013

ISBN: 978-1-4817-0599-8 (sc)
ISBN: 978-1-4817-0598-1 (e)

Library of Congress Control Number: 2013900402

Why should I look to another man to direct my Path
When he doesn't know his own path?

-Worrel A Edwards

Contents

Chapter 1: Try God

Chapter 2: God Answers

Chapter 3: No Greater Love

'

Dedication

Be alert, stand firm, be brave, be strong. Do all your work in love. May you find a place within you that brings comfort, peace and love.

Acknowledgements

Thanks to Jehovah

I acknowledge with love and happiness all my friends who encouraged me. Thanks to Beverley McKenzie for your continued support, thanks to my wife Donna and Priscilla my daughter. Thanks also to Denise my best friend and William Ashley my cousin, for cover designs and interior art. God's blessing is with you all.

Foreword

This is a message that we heard from the beginning, that we should love one another. (Ref. John 3:11). A message that resounds fundamentally in Worrel's work. Having become a child of God he has come to learn resolutely that love is the key to life abundant and eternal through Jesus Christ, who came not only that we may have life but that we may live it in abundance (Ref. John 10:10). A gift from God in the demonstration of His infinite love with a promised eternity: "For God so loved the world that He gave His only begotten Son, that whosoever believes in Him should not perish but have everlasting life." (Ref. John 3:16). Every believer (born again in spirit), has Christ living in them and also have received the love of God. (Ref. John 17:26).

The love of God as demonstrated by Jesus Christ is sacrificial and unconditional; it is immeasurable and eternal. The love of God is not limited to any human description, expression or understanding. It is too high, too wide, too deep and too perfectly complete to be fathomed by any human understanding or rationale. God himself by nature is love and true love can only be expressed with goodness; love is the bond of perfection which God requires that we all 'put on' every day of our lives. (ref. Col. 3:14). In other words, love is expressed actively and not in words.

We who live with God in us are privileged to the benefits of His fullness in which He indwells us. All this can be expressed through us continually, as situations and circumstances unfold in our lives. Living in faithful surrender to God, we allow Him to express Himself freely and soundly in and through us with inspiration, hope gratitude and love for a lasting impact which can only be accomplished in the grace of God, our heavenly father, by faith and through fellowship of oneness with Him. Our natural efforts at their very best can never achieve the excellence of God Almighty which is perfect love.

Living extraordinarily in God requires firstly that we in our acceptance of Him, should love our creator 'with all our heart, with all our soul and with all our might.' (Ref. Deut. 6:5).

God highly esteems our love and he also calls on us to love each other dearly: 'Love your neighbour as yourself.' (Liv.

19:18). Jesus Christ, the son of God who demonstrated the sacrificial, unconditional love of God for mankind, by willingly giving up His life on a cross for our justification and rising again from death that we might have victory, healing and life, tells us to love our enemies and bless those who curse us, to do good to those who hate us and pray for those who are spiteful—who persecute us. These exceptional acts of love described in God's word, inspire the life which Worrel typically perseveres before our eyes. 'Thoughtful Reflections' encourages us to put on love and to live it out daily in obedience to God as His children, as we may walk in the fullness of his grace and the abundance of His unfailing love which fuel and drive us to live in the way that we should live and operate in our responses and initiations toward others. We are 'lights of the world and salt of the earth.' (Matt. 5:13-14) and should live in ways that God's goodness is revealed before the eyes of mankind for His glory and praise.

That is the message that Worrel Conveys in this series of Spiritually inspired poems.

'Let Your mercies come to me O Lord—your salvation according to your word. So shall I have an answer for him who reproaches.' (Psalm 119:41-42 NKJV).

An answer with words full tasteful savour to reveal your glory irresistibly.

W. Ashley, Toronto, Canada.

Try God

Chapter 1

Teach me to love

Teach me to love O Lord
As I go through my daily chores,
Guide me O Lord I pray
As I go through my daily chores.

Each day that comes my way,
Give me strength to endure
The task that's set before me,
That I can love and show compassion
No matter what the task maybe,
I am depending on you.

Temptation is along the way,
Persecution and suffering
Is along the way,
But my faith is in you Lord,
I know you will rescue me
With your love and kindness;

Let us do our best;
The end of all things is near,
Let us love one another earnestly,
Jesus you died that we may live;
What a love you have for us.

Joyful

Let your hope keep you joyful,
Be patient in your troubles,
Pray at all times;
Have the same concern for everyone,
Try your best to love at all times.

Do not be proud,
Humble yourself like a child,
If someone done you wrong
Do not repay him with wrong;
Do everything possible to live in peace.

Don't take revenge
Let God do it instead,
God will pay back to everyone
According to his work.
If your enemy is hungry feed him,
Don't let evil defeat you.

A new start

Time for a change
What is done is done,
God has given me a new day
To start all over again,
I'll do it His way,
I will let go the past
And forgive myself of yesterday.

Lead me O Lord
In the right direction,
Even when am in doubt,
Let me remember
That you will never leave me alone,
Let your Holy Spirit
Fill me up with confidence.

It is hard to walk life's journey,
But give me strength
So I may not fall by the wayside,
Giving up is not on my mind
For I believe in you,
No matter what Lord.

Keep on going

When the road get rough
And the journey seems endless,
Remember Jesus is a way maker
Just keep believing in Him,
Keep on going,
He will see you through to the end.

Sometimes you'll feel like giving up,
For everything that you try
Seems to be going wrong,
But hold on to the Lord,
Keep your faith and dreams
And a positive note;

For this life is not an easy task,
The enemy will let you believe
You can't make it,
But with God,
All things are possible,
He said the world will hate you if you love Him.

All i've got is you

When friendship is on the line
What about trust, loyalty and respect,
When friendship is on the line
What about love,
Forgiveness and kindness;

God is all I've got
From my cell block,
These walls are my company,
I will never give up
Time is what I've got,
So I think about all the things
That I've done wrong.

I am still your friend
Even though you give up on me,
I have nothing bad to say about you,
I pray to the Lord,
To keep me safe from danger at all times,
I'm leaning on the Lord;

This is not a good place for any man,
Since I've been here
I've learnt about faith,
I've learnt about hope,
I've learnt to be humble;

A better day

Jesus there were times
When you let the world know
That poor and rich are equal
In God's sight,
One for all and all for one;

Your words give the people hope
For a better day,
That they can live on without giving up,
For you let them know that
We are one.

It doesn't matter what country you're from
We must try and live together,
Jesus stands for love;
Some may hate what He stands for,
But that is the price He pays to be who He really is,
The son of God;

Count your blessing

Everyone that I know
Is doing well except for me,
God what have I done?
I pray and my prayers are not answered,
I've lost faith in you
And I don't know what to do,
Why do you let me suffer?

I've come to the end of my rope,
Everything that I've tried, don't work for me,
What am I living for?
I'm no good at all,
I fail in everything that I do,
I don't want to live anymore.

Then I realitse . . .

Lord I am in good health,
I have food on my table,
Clothes on my back,
A roof over my head,
I have a family and friends who love me,
But I don't have the material things
That make me feel successful.

Count your blessings and be thankful,
Count your blessings and be grateful.

Constant love

Every time I think of killing my brother,
Remind me O Lord
Of your constant love,
Every time I think of killing my sister,
Remind me O Lord
Of your constant love;

Don't let Satan
Get the upper hand of me,
For you know what his plans are,
Temptation is all around me,
Give me self-control
That I can withstand the hands of the enemies;

Let me submit to you,
Righteousness and truth will be my light,
Darkness could never
Overcome your love,
Give me strength to overcome
The hands of the wicked;

Protect me in the morning,
Protect me in the evening
For I put my trust in you,
Never let me forget you,
Keep your light shining in me from dusk till dawn.

Children of light

Children of light,
Let your work
Shine upon the face of the earth,
Show that you really are a light.

Please God, and not man,
I've seen the work of men,
They're full of pride, envy and hatred,
Boast about their wickedness,
They are lovers of iniquity.

We the children of light
Must love like Jesus do,
Unconditionally;
Show our brothers and sisters
That Jesus is love,
Never turned His back on the poor and helpless.

He sat with sinners,
Never put them down,
Showed them love and kindness,
Teach them about righteousness,
I'm here as a servant of the Lord,
To follow in His footstep
Until my work is over,
Over and done;

Don't get lost

I don't want to get lost in religion,
And that's my decision.

I want to love a man
For whom he really is,
Regardless of his religious belief;

I don't want
To hate another human being
Because of his religion and that's my decision.

Can you love beyond
Your religious belief?
If you can't you are lost.

Man got lost the minute
They began to compete against themselves.
A man is just a man.

Destination

I think I've reached my destination,
I'm coming off,
Don't want to ride
With you anymore,
Pull over! make a stop for me,
I'll be alright.

I need someone
Who is going my direction,
The Lord's way
That's the way I want to go,
The road maybe rough,
The road maybe tough,
But I'll give it a try.

Tired of fighting with you,
Can't go on living this way,
I need some peace and love in my life
And only God can give it to me,
So I'll take a ride
On the King's highway with my Lord.

Dove

They say nothing good
Comes from Nazareth,
But the greatest man that ever walked the earth,
Comes from Nazareth,
Dove flies in the ghetto too.

Who is to be blamed
For the children that suffers in the ghetto?
They need tender loving care
Like any other children,
Dove flies in the ghetto too.

Even though we are facing
Crime and poverty,
I still see hope for the children,
Dove flies in the ghetto too.

God would never give a man
More than he can bear,
It's not easy living in fear,
Dove flies in the ghetto too.

Eternal strength

My sins make me weak,
I've recognised my faults,
It makes me sad
To hurt you again and again,
Like an addict looking for the next fix,
One excuse after another;

Lord give me the strength
To overcome my weakness,
Your forgiveness is not enough,
I need your eternal strength
To resist these feelings,
Help me to be strong.

Take away my weakness,
Make me strong again,
Let me be faithful to you and everyone
That I share my life with,
Let me be complete,
Let me be true to myself.

Easily forget

Man will never see the good that you do,
They easily forget the good that you do,
But always remember
The bad things that you do.
It's the bad things that makes them feel
That, they have something to hold you down.

The good you do for mankind
Is shortly lived inside the heart of men,
But never forgotten by God.
Look not to man for reward,
For the good that you do
Or you will be disappointed,
Do all things from your heart.

Man's love is based upon favour,
God's love is based upon truth,
Man fine ways
To justified the wrongs that they do,
While God finds all wrongs as wrongs,
So worship God as truth only.

Faith is the poor man's hope

Faith is the poor man's hope
For a better day,
When he loses faith
He loses hope leading to frustration.

Hate what is evil,
Hold on to what is good,
Hate what is wrong,
Hold on to what is right.

Temptation takes over
For there is no hope,
The devil takes over;
Faith is fading but God is there
To restore your hope and faith.

When frustration and temptation
Is all around you,
And faith and hope is hard to hold onto,
Just call on His name
He is the God of mercy.

Feel free

There is a love within me
That makes me feel free,
It is a love of goodness;
There is a love within me
That makes me feel free,
It is the love of God.

How can I go around
Hating my brothers and sisters?
Just because we are different
By the colour of our skin,
And a language you may not understand.

How could you say that I'm a racist?
When all I give is true love from my heart,
Can't you see that I love beyond religion?
I love beyond class and race
For, it is God that made us all.

Hate is blinding us
From seeing what is right from wrong.
We have to face the fact,
To learn to live together
Or just continue to kill each other,
We can learn to talk God's way.

Fear god

I have learned that,
From the day that I was born
I was also dying.
Each day that I grow,
I grow towards death.

I see death every day, yet I live.
Each day that you live
You get one day older,
From baby stage, to a child.

You grow from a child to an adult,
These changes shows
That you are one step away from getting old,
So to live in the spirit
Is to know Jesus.

The spirit never gets old.
The mind is so powerful,
It can take you places
You could never go in the flesh.
The spirit never gets old,
Just the body wears out.

God's blessing

God's blessing is at my feet,
But I'm too proud to bend on my knees,
I was just too blind to see
The way of the Lord,
Now I have given up my pride
And turned from my arrogance,
I'm trying to be humble in every way.

Now I am content and at peace,
My heart is quiet within me.
I've learn to live by His command,
It makes me feel a love that is true.
Since you've been in my life
I've seen the light of day,
My conscience is free,
The evil is still around but I'm under God's control.

God remembers

Remember, the love of God
Will never change.
If you are poor,
Men will treat you with no respect
As if you are less of a man.

The world sees the rich man
As a special being,
Don't let that get you down
Because you are poor,
Remember God is your
Light and salvation.

God will never forget the righteous,
He will remember you
From generation to generation.
The rich man's wealth is His salvation,
So don't worry
The Lord will guide you continually.

God will

I lost my way,
Now I find myself astray,
Things get so hard
That it makes me feel
Like I'm going insane.
It seems like it's going to rain forever,
But I'm not giving up.

God will let the sun shines
Once more in my life,
I'll make the best of it
In every way I can,
So I'm holding on,
I'm not giving up.

I know God will never
Let me down
But, I'm praying for His mercy
That I may have the strength,
To face each day and overcome each task.

God never gives up

Even through my weaknesses
God did not abandon me,
He gives me strength to carry on,
Even when the odds were against me,
And all I could see were obstacles
Everywhere in my way.

When it seems impossible
In the eyes of men,
And the mountain before me
Looks like a wall,
That is covered in grease with no way up,
God makes it possible for me to climb to the top.

God never give upon me,
God will never give upon you,
No matter what you are going through
God is there with you,
Look very closely and you will see Him
Helping you through.

God's constant love

I turn to you O Lord
Because I have no choice,
I've tried everything and failed,
I'm giving you a try in desperation.

Let your constant love
Comfort me,
Let your constant love
Be my guide.

I cannot chase after silver and gold,
Or diamonds and pearls anymore,
For the more I have is the more I want,
I would kill for it without remorse.

Nothing is complete
Without the blessing of my spiritual Father,
He fills the emptiness and makes me happy,
He is the love I've been longing for.

God is my strength

God is my strength and power,
He makes my way perfect,
God is my strength and power,
He is my refuge.

The Lord lives and blessed be my rock,
The rock of my salvation,
Who has lifted me high above them
That rose up against me,
I will sing praises unto His name.

He drew me out of many waters,
Delivered me from my enemies,
I know that the way of the Lord is perfect,
So I put my trust in him.

He will never let my feet slip,
Righteousness will be the path
He chooses for me,
To walk over hills and valleys
Upright in His sight.

Hidden hate

Who will believe me?
It's only the man that feels what I felt
That will believe me.
I see what the evil man can do,
Hidden hate a mask that smiles
And words that are smooth as silk.

I carry no grudge,
What you have done to me
It has already been done to you.
God said "leave all vengeance to him"
I am only here to deliver the message.

You try to break me and I almost fall,
But greater is he that watches over me;
No weapon that has been formed against me
Shall prosper.
I am protected by the Almighty God.

Hate is a poison

There is no place for hate
In the righteous man,
He forgives so that the spirit
Of God can live within.
The spirit of God, cannot embrace evil
But only embraces good,
So love can spring from you like a fountain.

It is the hate
Within a man that destroys Him,
God kills hate with love,
God kills evil with good,
Man kills himself when he hates.
Hate is a poison that destroys the mind,
The body and the soul.

Living in hate is living in hell,
Hate and evil are the roads to destruction,
Wickedness, greed and jealousy,
Murder, deceit and malice,
Hateful, proud and boastful,
You can't go on living this way
My brothers and sisters, we are all one.

Blind is their mind

They laugh at me saying
What good is your God?
You've got nothing to show from Him.
Blind is their mind,
Deaf is their thought;
They glorified what is useless,
And embrace what is evil.

The shadow of darkness blinds their eyes,
Yet they believe in
The things that they can only see,
But my God is only visible
To the good, not the evil;

He keeps them blind
From seeing His beauty,
And let them fall
In their own wickedness,
My God, my trust in you,
Keeps me safe from the wicked.

It's only god

Every time there is a problem
War seems to be the answer;
Give God a chance
He'll go the distance,
He has the resistance;

Remember, this world is our home,
There is no other.
God gave us to live in peace
And harmony,
But we chose to fight each other.

We chose hate over love,
We chose war over peace,
We turn our backs on God.
Envy, malice, greed and power,
Is what we chose instead of God's love,
It's only God who can save the world.

Lost humanity

The Lord looks down on us from Heaven,
To see if there are any who are wise,
To see who will worship Him,
But they have all gone wrong.

Mankind has failed, the world
Traded love of humanity
For a world of vanity,
So we've lose our sanity.

We are all equally bad,
None of us does what is right
We are all corrupt,
And done terrible things.

Don't we know that in all these evils,
Robbing and killing the humble,
We will answer to the Lord,
That protects the righteous?

Money

Money has become everything to people,
Love doesn't mean anything anymore,
All people care about is money,
If you have money, people will respect you,
Regardless of how wicked you are.

Some people say that it's the time,
But I say to these people,
Try and know God, for He is the time.

Without Him all things are meaningless,
Love God and live,
Hate Him and continue to do wrong,
And live in the house of evil.

I listen

I hear men quote the scripture
But their actions are all different.
What they say
Is not what they do.
They are all bitter inside,
But they can put on a good show
With their words.
They are full of pride, and
It eventually kills them.
Bitter with Hate;
Always doing things
To get the approval of man, and not of God.

Poor, wise, rich and foolish

It is better to live in a shack,
Than to live on a hill top in a fancy house;
With blood stains all over your hands.
It is better to be humble,
Than to be selfish and wicked.

Take a life or two,
To acquire your fancy clothes
And your flashy cars,
That is not what life is all about!
It's the way of the evil one.

If you can live on love,
My brother and sister,
You will live forever;
For the greatest achievement in life,
Is the blessing of God.

No fear

It is better to be poor and happy
Than to be rich and sad,
For the poor who know the ways of God,
Know, His blessing is the wealth
The foolish will never receive.

He who God leads will never stumble,
But will walk upright before his enemy
At all times, without fear of defeat;
For God has already set his path
Straight before him;

To trust the unknown, the invisible, supreme God,
Is to breathe the air without fear,
For the air exists, but is never seen,
If you believe, then you already know Him,
Just as you breathe to stay alive,
He is the air you breathe;
That allows us to move and exist.

Remember

The devil has a way
To lead us astray;
If you hear God's voice today,
Do not be stubborn.

The word of God is alive and active,
Sharper than any double-edged sword.
It cuts all the way through
To where, the soul and spirit meets.

It judges the desire and thoughts
Of man's heart,
There can be nothing hidden from God,
Everything in all creation
Is exposed before his eyes.

Remember, we must all
Give an account of ourselves,
So let us hold firmly
To the faith we professed;
For He is the high priest of all men.

GOD
Answers

Chapter 2

Hate is knocking

My friend has let me down,
I am feeling so sad inside,
But yesterday is gone,
Today is here; and those memories
Still linger on in my mind.

Lord, mend this broken heart
With your love,
That's the only way
I can be free from this pain,
That I'm feeling inside of me.

I need your comfort
So I can heal this broken heart,
Hate is knocking at my door,
Fill this heart with your love O Lord,
Don't leave any room for hate.

Help me o lord

Lord I've sinned against you and only you,
All my sins have caught up to me
I can't sleep well at night
All I do is toss and turn,
And it's only you, who can set me free from all my sins.
Renew my heart,
Fill my mind with only your thought, so I can be free.

What I love is killing me.
The sin's of this world
Have gotten a hold on me;
I am trying to let them go but it's so hard to do,
It's only you who can break me in two
And put me back together.
Separate me from this world, that is ruled by the enemy.

Close my eyes, and open up my mind to your ways,
Only your way can set me free, O Lord,
From the things of this world,
Including the choice of friend I choose.

I found you

Since I found you, Lord,
I find no pleasure in material things,
But I found joy in your salvation.
I was worried until I found success in you.

The success that comes from you
Is sweeter than honey,
More precious than money.
You made it known to me that it's not because I'm good,
But because of your mercy and your eternal love.

My problems are set before me like a mountain.
But I know you will help me
Step by step, through my entire problem.
You will give me the strength
To climb over this mountain.

It is impossible

It is impossible
For a man to believe
In the Lord and fail.
Believe not in me my friend,
I'm only here to give you encouragement,
With your faith.
You will receive your reward in the end,
God never fails.
He always proves that His love is true,
But we've never waited upon him,
We take things into our hands,
Then we say "I've prayed and nothing happens,"
But man's time and God's time are not the same.

I'm not afraid

I'm not afraid
Of what man will say,
I'm not afraid
Of what man will do,
For God will see me through
While I am doing his work.

They can put me down,
They can say anything,
That they want to say about me,
But as long as God is with me,
His work will be done through me.

I'll give what the Lord
Restored in me,
That's all I can give, it is true love,
To each and every one.
There will be no special treatment.

I slipped

In this life there is so much
Ups and downs,
I don't ask for diamonds or pearls,
I don't ask for silver or gold,
Lord, all I need is your love.

Many times I slipped
And you held onto me,
Lord give me the strength to carry on,
Shine your light that I may see the way.

Life's road is so bumpy, I stumble
But your love keeps me going on.
Your love helps me
To walk along the bumpy road;
Without it I know I could not make it.

I'm not a thief

Lord they want
To turn me into a thief,
Help me, O God,
To do the right thing;
It may cause me my job.
I know you are just
And fear in your doings.

Help me to get out
Of this wickedness,
Where man has no conscience,
They thief without any reason,
Just because of greed,
Don't let me be a part
Of their wicked scheme;

O Lord my God,
Let the wicked have
No control of me,
Take me away from them,
That my conscience maybe
At peace with you.

I will not rest

I will not rest!
I will prove to them
That my God is a living God.
Danger cannot harm me
For my God is real.

I don't know why
They want to see me fail,
Just because I'm climbing
The ladder of success,
But I'll put my enemies to shame.

One thing I know,
The greatest revenge is to love your enemies;
And that is the route I am taking
With God by my side.
I know I'm making the right choice.

I'm thankful

They can say, what they want to say,
They can do, what they want to do,
But they can't stop me from loving you.

Some say you are dead,
Some say you don't exist,
But I know you are alive,
Yes I know you exist,
For you woke me up this morning.

Lord I can't live without you,
I need you every step of the way,
Your guidance I need
To carry me through each day.
My love for you is getting stronger.

I will love you to the end of time,
Your name I'll adore,
Your name I will praise,
No matter what men say about you
Your're everything to me,
You are my Lord and Saviour.

I'm not for sale

I try to be humble
But evil flourishes
When a good man does nothing.
I'm going to do what is right,
In God's sight.

They could never buy me,
They try to but I'm not for sale,
My love for God makes me priceless,
I will not embrace evil.

I will speak the truth,
No matter what they think,
I don't fear wicked men,
For my God is with me
Every step of the way.

Why should I see
Things that are not right,
And pretend its okay
Just to get a break;
I would never sell my soul to the wicked.

I've done wrong

I know that I've done wrong,
Never said that am perfect.
I know that I've done wrong,
Just asking for God's forgiveness;

I'm sorry for everything,
That I've done wrong
To each and everyone,
God is my judge, and He is just,
He will not hold me guilty
For what I didn't do.

Before you cut me down
Look in the mirror,
There is no secret that He doesn't know of,
Pray that you may not fall by the way side,
Give love instead,
You don't know, what's awaiting you.

Don't sit around your table
Cutting your friends down;
The evil one's prayer has been answered,
Make time to give thanks
For all the good things,
That God has done for you,
Don't throw any stones, we all fall short.

I know you will be there

I've been down, and there was no one
To give a helping hand,
Temptation is knocking,
Hear my cry O Lord,
I'm way, way down.

Lord, I know
You will never forsake me,
Lord, I know
You will be there for me.

Lift me up with your grace,
This life I'm living
Is full of troubles,
And only you can take away my trials.

Lord, put me on solid ground,
Take me from this hell.
I don't want to be the one,
Crying from a jail cell,

Jesus never fails

When you feel
It's the end of the journey;
There is no one to turn to,
Friends are nowhere to be found,
Remember, you've got
A friend name Jesus.

When times are rough,
Love one's give up on you,
Jesus will be your friend,
He will restore everything that you've lost;
He is a true friend,
He'll never let you down.

When you're alone
And there is no one to talk to,
Family cut you off,
Turn their backs on you.
When tears are not enough to ease the pain,
Jesus will be there for you.

Lord i've failed

I didn't fail because I don't love you,
I didn't fail because I don't care,
I failed because I gave up on you.

Lord I failed because I stopped believing in you,
I've lost my way, O Lord,
When I turned away from you,
Leaning on my own understanding.

I am a man of pride
Don't want anyone to tell me what to do,
Don't need any help from anyone at all
For I can do it on my own.

I've made my own laws,
I am free to do what I want to do,
I don't care who I hurt as long as I am ok,
But the tables turned,
When I lost my health, I lost everything.

It is God, who gives health and strength,
And without health and strength
There is nothing I can do,
In the end I learn that God is everything.

Last days

Living in the last days isn't easy
No one seems to care anymore,
Every day people fuss and fight,
But revelation tells us, the bible is the key.
Open your eyes
To what the world is going through.

Remember what John said in Revelation,
All these words will come to pass
You know not your bible in this time,
You know not God,
For, He is the light out of this darkness.

Don't you know,
We are living in Revelation
And there is only one solution,
You've got to live for God,
You can't let the devil take control of your mind,
You will fall in the pit of wrath,
Without God, yuh done dead a'ready.

Life's mystery

I rise above my trials each day,
Faith carried me through yesterday.
I learn not to make
The same mistakes tomorrow;

I have the courage
To face each morning with **love**,
I give God thanks
For life and a **sound mind**,
My path that is set before me is unknown.

I don't let the unknown bother me
For it is life's mystery, that I cannot change.
It brings joy, it brings sorrow.
Whatever we do or say,
The results, we will have to live with.

I learn to put
My trust not in man,
But a **power** greater than man's mind,
Yet as humble, as the air we breathe,
It gives thought that changes all things.

Live your life

I learn not to worry
About what people say,
For I would end up living my life,
To satisfied their ways and not mine;

Man controls nothing,
But his own destruction,
The only way to avoid such things,
Is to let God be our leader, on this journey.

If you turn away from the Almighty,
You'll lose your way,
He is the light that keeps us safe,
So we will never stumble as we walk life's path.

Losing control

On my knees I pray O Lord,
Will you teach me to love?
It is so hard
When temptation is all around me.

I try my best to love and care,
But I lose it sometimes,
I guess it only takes a minute or two,
To hurt someone you love.

Sometimes you realize
When it's too late,
The damage is already done,
And sorry is the only thing
You can say; and hope
It can make amends.

Love

God created the human race
The human race created racism . . .
It takes love to change the world,
Unconditional love;
What kind of love do we need?
Unconditional love.

To find that love in your heart,
Go down on your knees;
Ask your heavenly Father
To teach you to love
With an open mind, for everyone;

Mankind, are you ready
To make that change?
First, you have to forgive;
If you cannot forgive
You're not ready
To make this world a better place.

Remember that God forgives,
He is a forgiving God,
We must do His will
To make this world a place of love
And happiness, to all mankind.

My mistakes

Lord, you give me
Everything that I needed;
You give me health,
You give me wealth;
Then I walk away from you,
For I thought I didn't need you anymore.

Now I lost it all,
My friends laugh at me;
My enemies rejoice,
I'm so ashamed,
I packed my things to run away,
But Lord, how far I can run from myself.

My sins caught up to me,
Lord I'm so filled with pride,
That I refuse
To seek your help.
Create a pure heart in me,
For I've recognised my faults.

The way maker

When times get rough
And it seems like you can't go on,
Don't you give up.
Even though you don't know
What you will eat or drink tomorrow,
Bless what you have today,
For God, will provide for your tomorrow.

Put your trust in God,
He knows about the bad times,
He knows about the good times.
Every day is a blessing.
No two days are the same,
So don't lose faith in God.

We know God is a way maker,
He will make a way.
No matter what the situation is,
He will see you through,
The good times and the bad times.
God is always there for you.

God be my guide

God be my guide;
My enemy is at my side.
Every stride I take
In my path they wait.

Protect me O God,
For in thee I put my trust,
I will set you O Lord,
Always before me
In everything that I do;

Keep me O Lord,
As the apple of your eye,
Hide me under your wings,
From the wicked that oppresses me.

Bless me O Lord,
Enlighten my darkness,
Let them fall;
Make my way perfect,
Guide me with your strength along my journey.

Father forgive me

Father forgives me of my sins;
I said I would change
But each day I make the devil
Take control of me,
For I keep doing the same things
Over and over,
Lord I am so weak, your strength I seek.

Give me your love in the morning,
Give me your love in the evening,
Let your love take me away
From all these things
That I am too weak to overcome.
I can't do it without you.

Let me see the light
That I may do the things that are right,
I am so tired,
I am so weak,
Your strength I dearly seek.
Will you break this spell
And save me from hell?

Be merciful

I've sinned against you O Lord
Over and over again,
Be merciful unto me O Lord;
Look away from my sins
Hold it not against me,
And I will be happy again.

Let your spirit of love
Guide me O Lord,
I can't fight this battle alone,
It is a spiritual warfare;
I'm fighting against the evil one,
Send your angels to protect me O Lord.

Angels of love; guide me
Through hate and bitterness,
Let me show love,
Let me give love, no matter what
Changes in life bring to me,
Help me to do what is right.

Lord build my faith for I am weak,
Give me the strength
To believe in you,
It is through faith that I will make it
Through to the end,
Lord through faith shall I live,
Only you can help me.

Give me faith

Lord, let your light shine on me
That I can teach.
Give me faith O Lord,
To spread your word.

Jesus is the light that erases
The darkness from my path,
I'm not afraid of the enemy anymore.
I will walk with this light wherever I go.
I'll never leave this light alone.

I will carry this light in my heart,
So when I speak this light flows,
From inside of me.
The truth from this light,
Cuts through any darkness,
That is set before me, each day.

No weapon can put this light out,
For it is the light that evil man fears.
Righteous man bows before it and humbles himself.
This light that lives inside of me,
Is the light of the true and living God.

Guide me o lord

Lord don't you leave me alone,
Because in this valley of darkness
You are the only one,
That can guide my path along the way,
So I won't get lost on my journey.

Some days when trouble come
And I feel so alone,
The pain is too much to bear.
You said you'll take my hand
And lead me to the light,
I know you'll never let me down.

Thank you Lord for the light,
Without it I would be lost,
Left alone in darkness.
There is no other like you
You're a true friend,
You'll never leave me alone.

Mighty king

O Mighty King!
You are the King of Kings
And the Lord of Lords;
The conquering lion
Of the tribes of Judah,
The son of the true and living
God Almighty.

I have been recruited into your army;
I am willing to serve you
In any way you want me to,
I'll bow down before you
In the morning;
I'll bow down before you
In the evening,
And praise your name always.

I'll be your servant,
O King Jesus,
And tell the world
What a good and great King you are,
And if you find me worthy, O King,
Of carrying out your work,
Reward me, King Jesus,
With humbleness and kindness;

My King and my Lord,
You have the power of kindness,
You have the power of compassion;
Fill me with them all
And then wash me all over with faith.
As long as I live, O Lord,
As long as I live, O Mighty King,
Let love flow from me,
Like a river of living water, that never runs dry.

Hold me in your arms

Lord, I don't want to hold onto
Your hands anymore,
For I keep on letting go.
I want you to hold me in your arms
And never let me go.

I don't want to go back
To the life I once lived,
Help me, O Lord,
From down on my bended knees I cry to you,
Please be merciful unto me all I've got is you.

You are my only hope,
Don't turn away from me;
Oh my saviour, forgive me,
I've learned my lesson, from walking away from you.
O Lord, open up your arms and receive me,
I am like the prodigal son coming home.

I'm feeling so ashamed,
But I put my pride aside and return to you,
I know you are the light, you are the way, you are the truth,
I want to walk with you forever and ever.

Wipe away my sins

Wipe away my sins, O Lord,
That I can pray;
So my voice maybe heard by you.
Hold not my sins against me,
For if you do,
All my prayer will go in vain.

Who can I depend on?
Who can I trust?
If you turn away from me,
I'll be lost forever;
So be merciful unto me, O Lord,
Let your Holy Spirit live within me.

No man can live without you
And be happy;
The only happiness,
I've ever known, came the day
That I started loving you.
My whole heart is delighted in your favour.

Glory be to the Lamb of God,
Worthy to be praised,
From the angels of heaven,
To mankind on earth.
He's worthy to be praised.

Don't leave

Please don't ever leave me,
Because in this valley of darkness,
You are the only one
That can guide my path along the way,
So I won't get lost on my journey.

Some day when trouble come
And I feel so alone,
The pain is too much to bear,
You said you'll take my hand
And lead me to the light,
I know you'll never let me down.

Thank you Lord for the light,
Without it I'd be lost,
There is no other friend like you
Sweet Jesus,
There is no other like you.

God is the answer

I'm tired am so weak . . .
Time stands still for me,
Nothing is going my way.
Everything that I do
Seems to be wrong.
God, will you keep me strong?

Each day that goes by
I need you more and more,
For every time I knock on a door
There is no answer.
I'm so frustrated,
Sometimes I don't know what to do.

Father, lift me up!
I'm down, way down deep;
There are no more doors to knock on,
I've knocked them all.
I'm knocking on your door, O Lord,
Please open your door for me.

God's time

Every time something goes wrong
We say, "Why Lord?
My Lord, are we worthy
To question you?

The sun is set on your time,
It rises each morning on your time,
Lord, it's your mercy
That allows me to see another glorious day.

Each day I see,
It's because of your love,
Let me have the courage
To face my tasks, one day at a time.

Help me to see life more clearly,
And appreciate the things that I have,
For it's you, O Lord,
That gives it all to me.

God is the light

In a world of darkness,
He was the light.
In a world of blindness,
He was their sight.

I believe in the gospel of Jesus,
He stands for brotherhood, peace and love;
Equality and justice for all mankind,
Jews and Gentiles.

He never turned His back on the poor,
Spread love everywhere he went,
His love is pure and true to everyone,
He is the teacher of righteousness.

Glorified by His Father in every way,
Truth is His name
Pure as gold, humble as a lamb,
He was crucified for the good He had done.

You've got a friend

God is everything,
And everything is meaningless
Without Him.
God is everything,
He is the beginning and the end.

When you're going through
Life's ups and downs,
Your mother and father forsake you;
Your best friend turns his back on you,
You're all alone;
Remember, you've got a friend.

When you lost
All your earthly possession,
And you have no one to turn to;
Tears are your only remedy
To ease the pain,
Remember, you've got a friend.

Sometimes when you feel like
The world is against you,
You don't know what to do,
Everyone lets you down;
You can't trust anyone anymore,
Remember, you've got a friend.

Chapter 3

My dream

In my dream
I've seen the light of love before me,
Like a rainbow,
Spread across the sky.
Oh what a beautiful sight,
I thank you Lord,
For changing my life.

It was peoples of all colours,
Class and race,
United before His presence.
It gives me great joy
To share this love;
I thank you Lord,
For changing my life.

It was more than words can say,
Love was everywhere;
We were like the ocean,
Colourless like water;
Embraced by His love.
I thank you Lord, for changing my life.

My protector

How can I live my life without God?
He protects me in the still of the night,
He wakes me up in the morning,
Watches over me all through the day.

Ever faithful, ever true;
Never let me down,
Can always depend on Him.
Always in my corner,
When there is no one to comfort me;
In time of trouble.

My enemy can never hurt me
For I put my trust in Him,
My life is in your hands that created all things,
He is everything to me,
He is my all in all.

No other like you

I know you will never
Let me down,
No matter what men say or do;
As long as I call upon you.

I'll keep on praising you day to day,
For there is no other like you.
My God, you are a one of a kind,
There is no other like you.

While you are around,
There's no one to take me down;
You're my strength,
You are my light,
You are my shield,
You are my protector forever.

Never let me down

Jesus . . . never let me down,
I'm depending on you.
I give you my heart,
I give you my soul,
I give you all that I have.

I believe in you with all my heart
Even though, the road is so rough,
And the burden is more than I can bear.
I pray O Lord, that you take away,
This suffering from me.

Keep me strong, that I don't do wrong,
Temptation is all around me.
The spirit is willing but the flesh is weak,
Your love I seek to carry me, O Lord,
Along the journey of life;

Don't let me fall by the wayside,
Give me strength to go on,
And continue to believe in you,
Day by day;
In this world of trouble and trials.

Original love

Do you believe in love?
If you do believe in love
You believe in God,
For God is love.

If you don't love
You are God's enemy,
If you know not love
You know not God.

Love is pure and so is God,
Love is patient and so is God,
Love never gives up;
God will never give up on you,
His mercy is so rich and his love endless.

If you believe in love,
You believe in God,
For God is love.
Father your love is original,
There is no other love like yours.

Our blessing

Yesterday is gone,
But Jesus remains the same;
Yesterday is gone,
But you are still here with me, O Lord.

We refuse to see our daily blessing;
There is not a day that goes by,
That we don't get a blessing from you.
We are so lost in yesterday.

Thank you for a sound mind;
Today is the day to give you thanks
For the life that you extend,
To live through this day, O Lord;

You let me see the sun shine once more;
The children play,
Food on my table, and roof over my head,
But instead, I complain, when I should be thankful.

Prince of peace

The devil is on a lease,
I don't want to be his tenant anymore,
I'm moving away from his desire.

Enroll in the army of love,
Enroll in the army of life,
Enroll in the army of the Prince of Peace.

When the rightful owner
Comes to take over,
I don't want to be there
Fighting against the Master;

Defeat will be the result for Satan,
So I'm joining the army of my Master,
To win the war.

Pray for our leaders

Judas was a disciple,
Do we condemn the other Disciples
For what Judas did?
No!
Do we condemn the church
For what the leader do?
No!
God is still in charge,
Don't you ever forget that
He is still in charge,
When we make mistakes
Or let earthly wealth possess us,
Then we know that pride has taken over,
And the evil one has taken control.
God wants us to be humble,
Let us continue to pray for our leaders.

Searching for love

Lord I'm searching for love;
Someone to hold me,
Someone to care for me.

Sometimes I feel like,
There is no love in this world;
Children are killing each other.

Something is missing from mankind,
Only prayer can restore it;
Look to the Lord, all ye nations, for His mercy.

I will put away my foolish pride
And look to you Lord,
For love and affection;
I know I will find it in you.

This love is salvation

Where there is love
There is truth;
When the truth is spoken
It is love to the soul.
Love must be above all things
And the truth above all things,
It's the breath of righteousness.

In the beginning the word was Love,
For God is love;
Love is the light,
Love is the way,
Love is the truth,
No man cometh unto the father,
Unless you accept true love.

This love walks among mankind,
This love stands for brotherhood and sisterhood;
It cannot be bought by any man
This love is not for sale,
This love is not carnal,
This love is free,
Your life must be controled by love,
Just as Christ loves.

God is over you

You can bribe the judge;
You can bribe the lawyer,
To set you free from all the wrongs
That you have done,
But can you bribe God Almighty?

You can have all
The body guards you need,
But one thing I would like to know,
Can they body guard your conscience
When you lay down at night and your
Wickedness surrounds you
And the blood of the innocent is before you?

No man can hide from himself,
God is over you;
You can't hide, you can't run,
He is everywhere and He will make sure
You get what you sow,
If it is good you will reap it,
And if it is bad you will **surely**, reap it.

The right way

The love I have inside of me
Is the love I can't resist.
Every time I think of doing
Something wrong,
It makes me feel sad inside.

Wouldn't want my sister
To hurt my feelings,
Wouldn't want my brother
To hurt my feelings;
So I think before I act
For love must be pure and true.

There is a right way
And that's the Lord's way.
Do unto others
As you would like them to do unto you,
Give love to receive love,
True love is like a river reaching out to sea.

True friend forever

I just can't get over you,
Friends for life.
That's what we use to say,
True friend forever.
Suddenly you left me behind;
Every now and then I think about you.

Sharing and caring for each other,
That's what we did best,
You never stopped loving me,
I never stopped loving you,
But I hope, my friend,
You are very happy.

It is so hard to carry on without you,
I hope we can work together
For the sake of the Lord;
And put our differences aside,
For if you walk without the Lord,
You will be lost.

True friendship

True friendship doesn't change,
When leadership and power is given to you.
True friendship doesn't change,
When God's love is guiding you
Every step of the way.

I admire your heart,
Not your riches.
Everything that is given to a man,
Will not last forever,
We are only here for awhile.

Show love and compassion
To everyone you meet,
Greet them with true love.
Don't use power and force unwisely,
There is one who watches over you.

Remember that all things,
Belong to God Almighty
And what you sow, you will surely reap.
All the power and the glory belongs to Him,
Humbleness is next to Godliness.

The good shepherd

While they get up,
Fuss and fight,
For the riches of this world,
I'm seeking the knowledge,
Wisdom and understanding of my father;
So I can spread the work of His son.

He is The Good Shepherd,
That gave His life for the sheep,
Children, don't be foolish, Jesus is the gate,
Don't listen to the hired man;
He is not a shepherd,
And does not own the sheep,
If he sees a wolf coming, he will run away.

I'm not working
For diamond and pearls,
I'm not working
For rubies and gems,
I'm not working
For material things.
I'm working for the love of God.

Something wonderful

People will throw your past at you;
Left, right and centre.
Don't let your past
Cause your life to end,
Let it be a reason for a new start,
Of something new and wonderful.

While they sit and talk and put you down,
Ask God to give you strength,
To do His will,
Mistakes are one of life's mysteries,
So rise above it.

What is done is done,
If you can acknowledge
What you do, you're on your way,
To be the best you can ever be.
Don't be afraid of what you cannot change;
Just be thankful that God forgives sins.

The creator

Without obedience
To His commandments,
No worship can be pleasing to God.
This is the love of God,
That we keep His commandments,
For he that turns away shall surely pay.

Remember He is the creator
And all that exist should worship Him,
For He is the one
That made us and not we ourselves.
Oh! Come let us bow down
And give Him praise.

Thou art worthy, O Lord,
To receive glory,
Honour and power,
For your mercy keep us going
From generation to generation;
There is no other like you.

26 Letters

Unity is what we need in this world today,
If we don't unite, things will never get right,
The alphabet is an example,
They all work together to make the first word.

Listen to me;
Together we can make love be our first word,
We can write it on our heart
The book of every man,
Children of all colour, class or race
Let us all embrace.

Look around us,
Tell me what you see
My brother and sister,
We are the twenty-six letters,
We need each other to make this world,
A better home for you and me.

Time out

We should take time out to see,
How much He really cares for us,
But we are too busy chasing the things
That bring no happiness to our lives.

Some fall short by the way side,
Blinded by the things of the world;
He never gives up on us,
He still reaches out
And pours his love in our hearts.

He is the Good Shepherd,
That watches over His flock,
With His love, He opens their eyes,
Guides them all from the wickedness of this world.

Undying love

Let us love the Lord,
With an undying love,
For His grace and mercy is eternal,
His love is the love of life.

Didn't God give you
Everything that you have?
How can you boast?
Who made you superior to others?
Where there is jealousy and quarrel,
We are not living right with one another.

Why do you think that
You are better than me?
Don't act foolish;
We are all God's children.
I may plant a seed, you may water it,
God is the one who makes it grow.

We are all equal,
Working together for God,
No matter what gift you have,
Jesus Christ is the foundation,
And no other foundation can be laid.
Let us do our best, set examples for one another

God is in control

Do you take the time
To see who is in control?
No nuclear weapon will have
The power over the human race,
God is in control;
We the children know.

We thought that oil, silver and gold,
Diamond and pearl,
Will give a man all the happiness that he needs
But we were wrong;
To know God's way is much greater.

The air we breathe,
It is more precious than all the wealth
That man stores away;
No man can store away the air,
If they do, how long will they last?
God is in control.

When i'm down

When I'm down
You comfort me
With all your strength,
With all your love;
That's what keeps me going on,
I could not make it without you.

Your love let me
Give a helping hand,
Wherever I go on the street,
The person I meet,
I'll greet with your love.

True love can change us,
So we see things we never seen,
Do things that we never dreamed
We could do:
Like going out of our way,
To help someone in need.

Love has the power
To make us feel good,
Does things inside of us
That we cannot explain,
Only you know that feeling,
I wish everyone could experience it.

Walk humbly

Why do we complain about the past
That we've created?
What is done is done,
Humble yourself;
Ask God for His forgiveness,
From the depth of your heart.

When the Lord forgives you,
Don't turn back
To your sinful ways,
Do what the Lord requires of you,
Act justly, love mercy,
And walk humbly with the Lord.

Let truth and peace be your guide;
It is love
That you should strive for;
Nothing in this world can compare to Him.

What a love

None shall escape
The wrath of God in this time;
For he gave us grace and mercy
Through his son, Jesus Christ,
That we may live in harmony.

He sits at the right hand of our father,
Pleading for you and me.
After all we have done
His love remains the same,
Unconditional love;
That's what he has for us.

He wants to give the world,
A chance to change
From our sinful ways.
Patient is he
Never holds us guilty
For the cross that he bore.
What a love;
What a friend we have in Christ.

How much more
Can Jesus love us?
How much more
Can Jesus care for us,
When his love for us
Is more than sand on the seashore;
When his love covers us,
Like the sky covers the earth.

Word power

It is the word that makes the world
Go round and round.
In the beginning was the word;
God commanded the word
And said let there be light,
And there was light.
Be careful what you do,
Be careful what you say,
For the words you speak,
Can make, or break you.

God who commanded the light
To shine out of darkness,
Hath shined it in our hearts,
To give the light of knowledge of the glory of God,
In the face of Jesus Christ;
Jesus ordered the spirit;
The people where all amazed
And said to one another,
What kind of words are these
With authority and power?"

Wake up with jesus

Tired of waking up each morning
With bills on my mind,
I want to wake up
With Jesus on my mind.

Going to bed each night,
All I think about are my bill to be paid.
Sometimes I feel
Like I'm going crazy;
Can't get enough sleep at night,
My mind is working over time.

Lord, I turn my bills over to you
From my bending knees.
Without a doubt in my heart,
I know, that you will
Never let me down,
The minute I call on you.

Even when I give up on you,
You'd never give up on me,
Your helping hands
Pull me out of all my troubles,
And turn my life around.
Now I can sleep at nights,
No bills to worry about
Because of you my Lord.

Where is the love?

We are the children of this world.
We are the human race.
Almighty Father,
Touch the leaders of this world;
Open their hearts and minds
To a love they can't resist.

Teach them, O Lord,
To understand that we are one;
And just as we came
Into this world with nothing,
So shall we leave.

Too many lives have been lost
For silver and gold;
Vanity has taken away
The love that should exist,
And leaves no love for humanity.

What an insanity.

Your love is true

Lord we say we love you,
Lord we say we would do anything for you;
But when vanity comes along,
How many of us will hold on to you?

We give up on you,
For the things
That we can see and touch,
Until we lose it all, to friends and family.

Now that I am down and out,
With no one to comfort me,
No one to talk with me;
It's only you that I see.

Lord your love is true,
Your love is everlasting.
Always forgiving,
With open arms you hold me,
Thank you Lord.

You'll be there

For me O Lord,
I know you will
Provide a cover when I am cold,
Shelter me from the storm;
Keep me warm.

I know you will
Be there standing tall,
To catch me if I should fall;
I know you will be my wall.

I know you will lift me up,
When the storm of life put me down;
I know you'll be around,
To pick me up from the ground.

I know my purpose

God, your love is amazing!
You've been good to me
Even before I've accepted you as my saviour.
When I was a sinner
You didn't give upon me,
You showed me mercy.

Changing my life style,
Doesn't mean I have
To change my purpose in life;
God's love has opened my eyes,
To see the world in a loving way,
I won't feel bad, I'll be glad.

If my purpose in life is to help
My brother and sister,
To make this world a better place,
I'll do it in the name of love
And only love.

God's love

For every beginning,
There must be an ending,
Except for God's love.
God's love for us has no ending,
For there is no beginning,
His love starts from within.

God, you love us first
With all your glory,
No matter what the circumstance is,
God, your love forgives and remain the same,
God, your love is everlasting,
Your love is eternal.

God, you gave us the earth
To live in peace—not war,
Your love must be our guide,
You teach us that forgiveness
Is the source of true love,
That's where your love starts,
And your forgiveness never ends.

Glory of god

The glory of God,
Is you, is me,
He love us more
Than we can ever imagine,
He has an undying love
For you and me.

He gave His son for the world.

The glory of God,
Is Jesus Christ,
The Lamb that died
To save us all,
So that we may walk upright
Before His presence,
That we may live in His light;

The glory of God,
Is to praise Him, honour Him
And love Him with all our heart.
Trust in Him, in all our deeds,
Have faith in Him,
Never forsake Him.

Thank you Lord.

God smiles

God smiles with me today,
For He has given me another day.
Yesterday seemed impossible to get through,
But His grace brought me through,
Everything that was not possible for me yesterday.

God smiles with me today,
He has given me a sound mind,
He gives me strength,
To withstand the entire problem that faces me;
Strength I did not know I have.
He proves to me that he still loves me.

God smiles with me today,
He lets me control my situation.
Never lost control, even when I was afraid.
He gives me the strength to carry on,
Who is like my God?
He is always there for me.